NOMENCLATURES OF INVISIBILITY

NOMENCLATURES OF INVISIBILITY

Mahtem Shiferraw

AMERICAN POETS CONTINUUM SERIES, NO. 200

BOA EDITIONS, LTD. § ROCHESTER, NY § 2023

First Edition
23 24 25 26 7 6 5 4 3 2 1

For information about permission to reuse any material from this book, please contact The Permissions Company at www.permissionscompany.com or e-mail permdude@gmail.com.

Publications by BOA Editions, Ltd.—a not-for-profit corporation under section 501 (c) (3) of the United States Internal Revenue Code—are made possible with funds from a variety of sources, including public funds from the Literature Program of the National Endowment for the Arts; the New York State Council on the Arts, a state agency; and the County of Monroe, NY. Private funding sources include the Max and Marian Farash Charitable Foundation; the Mary S. Mulligan Charitable Trust; the Rochester Area Community Foundation; the Ames-Amzalak Memorial Trust in memory of Henry Ames, Semon Amzalak, and Dan Amzalak; the LGBT Fund of Greater Rochester; and contributions from many individuals nationwide. See Colophon on page 92 for special individual acknowledgments.

Cover Design: Sandy Knight
Cover Art: Kokeb Zeleke
Interior Design and Composition: Michelle Dashevsky
BOA Logo: Mirko

BOA Editions books are available electronically through BookShare, an online distributor offering Large-Print, Braille, Multimedia Audio Book, and Dyslexic formats, as well as through e-readers that feature text to speech capabilities.

Cataloging-in-Publication Data is available from the Library of Congress.

BOA Editions, Ltd.
250 North Goodman Street, Suite 306
Rochester, NY 14607
www.boaeditions.org
A. Poulin, Jr., Founder (1938—1996)

For Kokeb, with love

So when we are given new names
our ears are closed shut
alien, immigrant,
it was as if they said,
sunflower, sunflower,

why, yes I am,
and I bloom at my pleasing.

Contents

The Eucalyptus Tree I
after Susan Hahn

I long for it on quiet nights and call it
home. It stands tall and muscular
above the mountains. It sees me
but does not flinch. It feeds me
honey and wild winds. It calls me
child, though I do not hear.
Its leaves, a balm for blistering skin;
what comes after a cry, or bleeding?
Its aroma, like autumn, like rain,
stands green, translucent thing,
between my father and I, and the ghosts
of Gojam. It sees us; bleeding
We carve wombs throughout its roots
and rest our little bodies. We bear
children the size of seeds and fold
them into our branch arms. The rings
of fire that embrace us are blue with fear.
Everywhere we go, we smell of death
and something sweet.

Nomenclatures of Invisibility

My ancestors are made with water—
blue on the sides, and green down the spine;

when we travel, we lose brothers at sea
and do not stop to grieve.

Our mothers burn with a fire
that does not let them be;

they whisper our names,
nomenclatures of invisibility;
honey-dewed faces, eyes sewn shut.
How to tell them
the sorrow that splits us in half,
the longing for a land not our own,
the constant moving and shifting of things,
within, without—

Which words describe
the clenching in our stomachs,
the fear lodged deeply into our bones
churning us from within,

and the loss that follows us everywhere:
behind mountains, past oceans, into
the heads of trees, how to swallow
a tongue that speaks with too many accents,

when white faces sprout,
we are told to set ourselves ablaze
and this smell of smoke we know—
water or fire, or both,

because we have drowned many at a time
and left our bodies burning, or swollen, or bleeding,
and purple. This kind of language we know;
naming new things into our invisibility
and this, we too, call home.

Lit

Incandescence is a name I inherit
from sultry ancestors; they must see
a light I do not see, and call me lit.
I grow dark underneath, as if I am
made of tired shadows, all intersecting
into each other, into another. We are
iridescent: black on black on blue
with slightly golden edges. We walk
in unison too: our backs bending at once,
our arms breaking, our abdomens
kicked into silence, thighs bleeding. Through
this, I ask: am I still lit? And they, again,
wave braided hairs in the same direction,
as if to say, what else would you be—

For Micah, My Neverborn

The day you came to me in thought,
I found myself at a crossroads, the word

of God supple in my mouth, a light I once
knew combing through the windows. You were

my prophecy, my bearing, my salvation.
It was you I saw first before the darkness.

I smiled a new smile, cradled my belly as if
it contained gold, tried to hide my newfound joy

away from everyone. I penciled you in my body,
created intricate paths for you to take, hand in hand

with my daughter, who would be your shield in the world
outside of me, she made of steel and so much joy.

I don't know how to think of her without thinking
of you: both have mapped this body and left it

empty and bleeding. It seems cruel to feel anything
but sorrow in your absence. I drank so much water

thinking this body to be a tree, thinking I could summon
it into nurturing you, slowly, slowly.

I named you, I knew you before it was so,
eating enjera dusted with berbere, shiro and firfir

believing this seed would need to survive
the spices of my ancestors to grow strong.

How foolish of me to think you would be made whole,
how foolish of me to keep hoping, even after your heart

stopped beating. I wanted to build you, construct you
bit by bit, make a home for you where there could be none.

But this body keeps housing wars that show up
unannounced. I have trained myself to wear armors

made of metal, to embalm myself with honey and
eucalyptus leaves. I have known ancient wars,

and wrestled them free from myself. I have torn this body
inside out, so it can shape itself into something new.

But you, I had seen you, and this seeing blinded me,
it sank deeply into my bones.

I don't know how to do this, how to continue
carrying with me a body riddled with new wars.

I don't know how to bear the wars of other women—
mothers, grandmothers, aunts, sisters—our language

is that of dying. I had so much to tell you, so much
to give you. This is when I finally learned to be free

with myself, to be generous, when I finally knew
how to be kind to this body. And then—you,

the weight of you, the knowing, carrying your death
inside of me for so long. The decisions afterwards,

all the incisions, sharp things going through
where your head would've emerged. The sound

of vacuums, the absence of a new cry, somewhere
a bag collecting you, my silence during all of it—

counting backwards, backwards, focusing on the
fluorescent lights, the lights, the lights, the lights.

In the aftermath: the thirst, the body not knowing
itself to be this vacuous; my bones brittle with sorrow.

I have done so much leaving before;
leaving my lands, leaving my body, leaving my family—

but this, I don't know how to leave this,
I don't know how to leave you, even when

you're already gone.

Who will know your name, who will remember
you now, who will keep your memory alive

if not this body, if not this sorrow? Yes, here,
grief has finally found a home.

At night, when the world is quiet with ancient
silences, this body unfurls and leads me
to new waters.

Here, I rest, beneath rivers that cross small cities
thinking of you, naming you, once more.

Sawdust

Here he stands, born to the befores,
now a boy, now a man, now nothing.
I am there with him, girl or other.
We are made with the same thing, and
we hum quietly. He is a fish too, telling
his daughters stories of men with lurking eyes.
We swim elsewhere and find him staring
into the open skies. He asks, what are we
doing here? He asks, are we really here alone?
I do not know what to say; he has become
a thing I cannot recognize. It's difficult to know
how many times he has lived before, ancestor
or descendant, or nothing more. When he comes
to me, he is immersed in deep purple, a slash
of oxblood rippling through. Perhaps he hasn't
lived this life before; the dark blue he has known
himself to be is but a thin gray, and his emeralds
are imprinted on my mother—sawdust upon her body.

The Languages I Speak

The languages I speak come to me
in my dreams. One is a serpent, but
I don't know which one. Toothless
and with blue venom, it enters my veins
and I let it breathe black blood. We become
one. When we shed our skin, we stand,
suddenly naked and alone, our bellies
bloated with thousands of words
we do not recall. We call this learning;
the learning we do takes years to muster
and never leaves. One is an empty cloak,
but its only red eye is turned backwards.
It does not see us, or it does, and we do not know.
The hissing sound we hear is not new, but slowly
inhabits our ears, our movements. On cloudy days,
it sounds like music too, but do not let it
fool you. We do not ask where we fit within the cloak—
inside or out. One is a cloud that refuses to rain;
this one drags itself behind us, its body the exact
shape of our shadows, and though fuchsia, or burgundy,
we know it is also of a bleeding shade. Its mist,
an old horror coming back home. And this one:
this is absence, the smell of something missing,
or mad. Both. It does not leave, and somehow
we find it hidden everywhere: a toothache we
cannot get rid of.

The Etymology of Fears

Something cold and unhinged swelters,
crawls underneath the skin, basin of a home

within this body. The scent of it, reminiscent
of things we once loved and lost: cardamom,

cinnamon barks, black and red teas, the sponginess
of *enjera* kneaded into foreign flours, *defo dabo* soaked

in *mitmitá*, pulled and tossed afterhours, when no one else
is around. We hold this: the dread of carrying old spices

within us. We learn to muster new things into new lands;
we nurse old wounds and turn them into silences. We do not know

our own exactitude; only the terror of the leaving, or being
left behind. We fear not knowing, or, knowing too much, or,

the horror of seeing too much too soon. We trace our origins
back to our ancestors, and wonder why they never spoke

of these gut-wrenching fears. We labor and labor to define them
accordingly; we build bridges to connect them, to contain them.

We hold on to our yearnings, our ancient longings, but the fear
is always there: the fear of having to shed too much blood,

the bottomless fear of being assimilated. We grow into the thorns
jabbing our ribcages, trails of purple and water everywhere we go,

and everywhere else: the fear of being called an alien, belonging
to neither world, this being a language we already know, a precise

sense of existence we can be contained in—the etymology of our fears enshrouds us once again in invisibility.

Wuchalle

*The Treaty of Wuchalle was signed in 1889 by the Italians and
Emperor Menelik II of Ethiopia, whereby the Italians claimed
protectorate over Ethiopia.*

May 2, 1889. Whereby the Italians granted
northern Ethiopian territories back to Ethiopia.

The word of note here being granted, which
leads one to think: the Italians, in Ethiopia,
granting anything, which implies: permissions,
relinquished.

The territories granted: Bogos, Hamasen,
Akele-Guzai, Serae, northern Tigray. If you didn't
know it yet, this also includes modern-day Eritrea.

Eritrea, which means, in association with
its Greek origin, Erythraia, or Ἐρυθραία,
and its derived Latin, Erythræa.

Which refers to the Erythræan Sea, the
Red Sea. It seems a matter of pure logic,
but here, it is not. Language is a thing
as malleable as history itself, which
leads me to this fact, or (non)fact:

the Italians being credited with creating
the colony of Eritrea. The year being 1890.

The word of note here: *creating*, which
implies, among other things, authority,
ownership. To be able to set across the ocean,
across unnamed seas and other waters, and
lands, and suddenly, having arrived at the

coastal states, suddenly not noticing
the existing communities, and instead,
deciding to take ownership—like that,
like that.

This is a familiar narrative,
but I will tell you anyway:

the privilege that comes
from planting one's flag
in a new continent,

the privilege of ownership
with language first—defining
the waters, the land itself, then
everything else;

the arrogance of being able to ignore
any pre-existing communities,

which I am inclined to call *indigenous*
but, that too, is a language of ownership.

Advancing as far as Wuchalle
before deciding which port, which
sea to claim—*all of it, all of it.*

Drafting a new agreement, the
Treaty of Wuchalle, in Italian first—
here, again, the language of ownership—
relinquishing territories for money and provisions;
thirty thousand muskets, twenty-eight cannons,
this being the value of such territories,
the value of such people.

Based on the treaty in Italian, claiming
the entire lands—mind you, an empire
as old as the Romans—claiming this,
and everything in it, and between it,
every mountain, every bleeding river,
every person, every tree, every unearthed
resource—claiming all of it: the language used:
protectorate.

Which means to define the relationship between two states,
one of which has control over the other.

Short of being a colony,
I cannot find another word to describe this state of being,

which leads me to believe, there is no word
for protectorate in Amharic—here again,
ownership, ownership.

Here, I must pause, and tell you
about the ancient empire of Abyssinia,
although historically well documented
I am inclined to believe you will not know
of it, or understand the complexities of this matter
until you fully grasp its pre-existing history.

Here, I am choosing to change the narrative;
here, I must give space to the Ethiopian
without rivaling with other narratives, here
is where you learn the story of a black kingdom
without a white conqueror.

Here, is where I grant you knowledge
even if briefly, here is where I equip you
with something new; here, I expect you
to go out in the world, and reclaim my
narrative.

Before we begin, note:
the first mentions of Eritrea
exist through the Westerners—through mentions
in 1st century AD Periplus of the Erythraean Sea—
a document tracing the trading and navigation by the
Greeks and the Romans—

and before we continue
I must warn you:

the stories of Eritrea
and that of Ethiopia
happen on different trajectories;

both lands claim my flesh;
and since I long equally
for the bleeding sea and the white-blue river,
I must serve them right
in telling you their stories;
(like twins split at birth
they are forever in search of each other,
and yet not).

We begin in the Land of the Punt,
2900 B.C., trading with ancient Egyptians;
then to Daamat, and to the kingdom of Aksum.

Here, I must pause again, to tell you about this land,
and this kingdom, that housed myrrh and gold,
that traded as an equal power with the ancient
kingdoms of Rome, Persia and India, that stretched
as far as the Arabian Peninsula, across a bleeding sea,
that adopted Christianity around 320 A.D., but also
welcomed the First Hijra, with a lineage that can be traced
to the Solomonic dynasty, a land that is the resting place
for the Ark of the Covenant.

Here is an empire that erects the obelisks of Aksum
25 meters granite stele, bearing portals to other-
worlds; and though these monuments have stood
since the 4th century A.D., somehow one finds its way
to Rome, dismembered and shipped through the Red Sea,
to commemorate the illusions of imperial Italians—

and how this very act, this disassembling and assembling
of stones, of bones, is carried without thought,
the thought being: the possibility of an African kingdom
defeating the white Italians; the afterthought being a question
shaking pure logic; how to then still think of the African,
the Ethiopian, as a savage—

how, almost sixty years later, somewhere in the 1990s,
not having been returned, the stele that is, having been
the constant question of Ethiopians, the Italian
government deciding to build a hospital in the city
of Aksum instead, as if that would right
the wrongs of its soldiers—having to dismember it
completely, unroot it from its land of origin, and
ship it seas apart, having to install it, proudly, in the
middle of a Roman piazza, its grace or historical
significance forever changed, having become
an ornament, a reeking bounty of war.

My Italian friends not understanding
why we would want an old and damaged
monument back, not seeing, this:

brokenness, brokenness—

and even then, being fascinated by
their quiet complacency of ownership—
telling us what to do, how to feel, which
story to erase. Having to meet their president,
Oscar Luigi Scalfaro, having to ask him,
in public, in perfect Italian, when we would see
the return of the obelisk; having to witness his surprise,
having known the answer before he said it—

Here is a land that stood the temperaments of time:
endless kingdoms, hundreds of monarchs, two fire-
empresses, numerous wars and into the 1880s,
to find itself facing the arrogance of ownership
from a white ruler across the seas,

and refusing to accept its newly found
protectorate status, refusing this new ownership,
its language, its caricature,

rejecting completely the treaty, then,
deciding to unite its armies—monarchs
from the north and the south—into the
Battle of Adwa, 1896, which means
six or seven years of swaying back and forth,
back and forth, such tenderness, such force,
the knowing of white men's cruelty
before they disembark in a "new" land,
the unknowing benevolence of my people,
savages, indigenous, black, black things—

and I, every year, having to celebrate
the commemoration of the Battle of Adwa
within the Italian School, having to explain
to white professors, the wrongdoings of their
ancestors, of their kingdom, having to
remember it all, Wuchalle, Aksum, Adwa, Asmara,
Massawa, The Red Sea—bearing things on our shoulders,
like this, like this,
allowing ourselves to speak in Amharic,
to sing like *arbegnoc*
to burst ourselves free into the shaking dance,
like that, like that,
like a thing went wild
the one day we embody all of it—
portals of ancient kingdoms, luminescent
all over our bodies, suddenly spewing outwards
the insidious ways of ownership.

Visions from a Late Grandmother

I see you adorning the corners of our
faces, voice seeping through quiet shadows.

When you move, we stand together, as if we were all
weaved through each other—letting you through
is our first act of imagination.

You pull up a chair and sit, pour *siwwa*
in white glasses wreathed with blue.

What you want to say cannot be learned
with these words. This kind of tenderness

leaps only from your eyes, sharp brown irises,
and the steel in your bones. We drink it whole,

though we are not allowed to do this, and other things,
among men. You are our foretelling of what small

acts of transgression can do to a woman, to a generation
of women-mothers, motherless women. Some things

we learn without our knowing—how to hold a
sleeping child, how to wash the brother's

favorite shirt, beating the dirt and blood out of it,
how to etch small emblems on white socks,
one for each of your fleeing sons,

how to shave our heads in mourning, empty craniums
commanding the skies into such softness. With each of our

children, you mark the lines of new continents
and break them open into rivers, lakes, and mountains

with lips of fire, all of this tender tearing apart
teaching them, and us too, the affliction

of running and running, never knowing
which lands would drink us whole,

never knowing the fear, the trembling of our fathers
who imagined us into this kind of submission.

The Eucalyptus Tree II

Let's call it father: it sees me be
but does not leave. Once, it was just
a seed, inhabiting a land beyond the seas,
and finding its way into the shoes of a king,
having been stolen, having crawled underneath
into our mountains, before it was so.
Let's say it illuminates my way, when it
is quiet and cold outside, and the shivering
is new with the laughter of spotted hyenas, and
I run to it, thinking it to be a thing I recognize, a face
that once looked at me as if I was whole
and split me into smaller pieces, and this running
is neverending; where else does one go
to smell of home and wanting?   Let's say,
it calls me daughter, and paints me gray;
on rainy days, I can hear its rattling, a soft purling
of leaves, and nothing more, housing things
I forget to give myself: new blossoms,
the singing of new birds, honeycombs thick with Spring.
And then, thinking it a mother, I curl myself on top of its head,
and the wounds I carry with me ripen and blister quickly,
for this is where I come to find myself
and die quietly, among leaves first grown
in a king's court.

Nomenclatures II

Those which we are given
in the brink of sorrow,
or joy—or both;

those marked on our foreheads
the curse of a generation,
or more,

marked on our abdomens
birthmarks, like numbers
aligning us with a history
we seem to forget;

those we carry within
years later, many lands apart,
having something rotten
from the inside out
our bodies finally drooping
with the weight of the firmament;

those we carve new and milky,
pasty on our foreign tongues
monosyllabic, odd things
reminding us of everywhere,
of nowhere;

those we receive, or hear
and not dissent to, shaping themselves
from our hair, the silhouettes of our
bodies, the color of our skin,
the foreignness of our mouths;

and those filled with grief
and strife—the names of our fathers
and foremothers, beaming through
centuries, across black seas
and into new lands, carrying us
throughout, containing us—

containing this, *all of it*,
all our names and naming,
calling us with something
filled with grim love.

Dust and Bones

Stranded at sea, bubble from
the earth, dust and bones
slide on my face.

This is not my story;
but in it I stand
called by other names;
the ghosts of my past selves
all reaching at the same time
and all refusing this—
this foreignness they smell
like something burned and tossed.

I dream of covering my body
with the white salt of Assab's dunes—

even Lot's wife
whispered the name of her city
with her last breath.

Instead, this body is bone,
made to fracture into multitudes,
black mud or dust
splintering my sides
here, there, here,

this, a new beginning,
a new death.

Auguries

Things leave his body and reshape
themselves in the room. We know
not to make a sound. One minute he sleeps,

the next, he jumps up, flickering,
eyes black with fury. Our bodies know then

not to breathe, not to move, and to instead
remain invisible, behind closed doors.

We shrink into small objects, thinking this
will save us from being noticed.

But these spaces bear the sights
of his demons; tables with dangling feet,
windows cracked, doors slammed shut,
a rupturing of things,

like the sight of my brother picking up
a stone, the body of my mother behind him,

and a fleshless wrath seeping through
father's beautiful, black hair.

The gunshots are a welcomed interruption
in this silence, his breath reeking of *areke*

and *tej* afterwards, words slurred, eyes
bloodshot. Finding a new courage to carry small

stones in my pocket for weeks, and the plotting
of escape routes. The horror of feeling such

tenderness at his sleeping, drunken body,
of returning to it all, as if

we did not harbor the leaving for so long.
Our bodies learn not to breathe, even years

later, suddenly recognizing the fury of quiet men
commanding us into submission.

The Breaking

I was born
with grief already etched
deep into these irises;

my skull heavy
with the smell of dying.

Everywhere I go
I see

someone waiting
to break me open
and scoop me out.

This breaking
is but a cavernous blue;

in it, the dancing of my mothers
and my mothers' mothers
is deep with yearning,

and we sing quietly
knowing the things we know,
constructing ways to safekeep
our children, our children's children,

in it. We sleep,
uneasily so;

the sleep
within the breaking
is never really sleep
until it is—

How to Measure Solitudes

Start as if sleeping pendulous
upon the mouth of a mountain,
glowing insides, the luminousness
sharpened with new things.

You think you might
smell death, but it is only
lavender, or sunflower seeds
on a cloudless day.

Then, travel following small trails—
these rivers are like restless spirits
who welcome you in every land
by an act of drowning
which you are inclined to believe
is out of mercy.

These things will color you
with new horrors; sanguine purples,
salmon blues, larva greens, and lurid yellows,
underneath all of it—too many to contain
in one you.

You may place them upon one breast,
as this one already reeks
from the sorrow of silences,
the horror of long distances.

You may also find it in hiding,
somewhere between your legs,
or flowering from the inside out
in your belly. When you look up,

clouds are shaped with it, and someone
stirs it into existence, the breaking of skin
already new.

An Exodus of Things

Here, our movements
are mapped within,

our fears, an exodus
of things.

Today, we fear our names,
or betray our ancestry, or
lose the nuances of this language,
that walk, this food, that particular scent.

The lands we occupy, the lands
we cross into, the lands
we set free
are too many to count.

The stories of our shifting
the bones to our being,
seas that assemble our old names,
boats bloated from our blood
from years of crossing, and crossing.

It is strange to think of ourselves
like this, like fleeting beings
without the wrath of flesh in
our bodies. We sit by

small trees, and give our children
the name of things
we couldn't bear;

summoning them as if
they are already made with fire,
and perhaps they are,
insisting they learn
how to speak properly, how not to carry
too many accents, how to exist ferociously
within the politeness of black bodies,
and moving bodies, persisting
in a white, white world.

We say this, "Do not forget
how once you lived
in a house made of mud
and starved to feed your family
and saved yourself only with prayer."
This, we repeat, over and over
again, until it is etched
deep into our collective bones:

Once, before all of it,
before the exodus of things,

we tell them,
you were, someone too,
we were, someone too.

The Markings

We have been mapped before, our bodies
turned into stone, drenched in myrrh
and thick incense, yearning no more.
We hold shadows within, count our graces,
our markings, new mercies we have been
granted through invisibility: a new gifting.
We have come to rest, here where we find
names to our broken pieces, where the lines
are drawn upon our chests, new waters
springing this way, that way, towards the fires
we have been taught to run away from.
Here, we are split: strings of veins, organs
pulping of life, the mess of it all—such beauty,
such tenderness. We are clipped together,
or patched, or misshapen so—and we see
ourselves everywhere—now on another body,
now imprinted on mountain tops, now on the
invisible walls of nameless cities.
What is this new longing we have been
cursed with? Where does it end? Then:
we are folded in half, as if we are made
of paper, griefs and sorrows abandoned
in old, old memories.
Here, consume us whole; find what
we cannot get rid of, and make us
bleed again. Here, here are our new
markings: new cartographies filled
with aching, and then, what are we?
What are we?

The Silences

Ancestor mothers approach
slowly. They are silences I have assumed
in my body. They speak a language I
have learned to hide deep in my bones.
They call me daughter, but I am also
a mother. In this, we all interchange,
dark-blues and blue-blacks, lustrous
greens adorning our kinks. Each of them
hands me something to misremember: a seed,
the beginning of a wall, a black dress,
a child, a white *netela*. See me afterwards:
my head is shaved, body thin-cracking,
limbs long, and large. I open my mouth and hiss
in a language I do not recognize. They wash
my mouth with cacti and let me drink their milk.
They call me daughter, again; and again, I say,
I am a mother, but do not know how to stop.
They feed this flesh honey and *kitta* and warm milk;
they sow my wounds and cover my scars with palm leaves.
They call me *adey*, *abeba*; and I am, small
and stubborn and yellow-green all over.

The Eucalyptus Tree III

Birch bones, feet sprawling
you contain me
in my liquid self;

this seed I had in me
how did it get there,

how did I not know
the grief of not being able
to bear lovely fruits?

I want to know
how to let myself fall
in a new learning.

This and more you see

bringing rain
from the yellow city,

dirt and bone dust
from the white city.

Here I am home
among quiet ghosts

something tossing
and turning inside

strange black hands
delving deep
where I do not belong.

Crossings

The lands we contain in our bodies
are too many to count.

This limb has been in the Pacific
and came out skeleton dry.

This hand has touched a face
so ashen it transcended the skies.

These feet have been running and running
until they were adorned with blisters,

the bearings of the nomad's life.

When you are asked
whether you are an immigrant or a refugee
say you're both, part of you belonging
here and there, and finally, nowhere.

How do we separate
this kind of grief
that has us always running,
always looking behind our backs,
always reaching for our passports,
always bloating at sea,
always bleeding, bleeding, bleeding—
always on the brim of death?

Tell them
these bodies are worlds
and our aching the maps
containing them all.

These limbs have already been
where no one ought to go

These eyes have seen
the dark shadows of entire continents

and what we have left: only
the solace
of blue winds.

The Slaughter

Perhaps we were taught to run away
from things like this, or perhaps we weren't;

I forget which one. I forget this too:
how terrifying each time will be,

their gazes all aligned, as if they belonged
to the same being, thinking us to be nymphs

lost in riverless beds. By this, we know to expect
the slaughter, and though our deaths are

not new, the dread will always break us open,
our small selves drooling out of despair. Only

mourning will do here, and singing, and singing,
songs to collect our misremembering, and pour them

onto the bones of our daughters, and our granddaughters,
because without this kind of exacting, there is nothing

left to do, nothing else left to be.

Assembling the Bones

These women are like small lights
guarding the portals of my imagination,
and this must be

a grandmother, or a great-aunt,
and though she looks exactly like me

or I like her, she looks like the others too
the faces of many resting on her,
bosoms heavy from heaving,

their bodies sour from learning
and unlearning deep-planted sorrows.

They bend, their backs fluid
with sanguine joys; this, they do
to survive, for they must see me already
and my pen that writes them.

They assemble the bones, I tear
open the flesh. Their obedience is
like fire in my stomach, and I see it, too,

the longing for this freedom to exist
without turbulence, without fear.

Beginnings

This is not how it begins
but how you understand it.

I walk many kilometers and
find myself to be the same—

the same moon hovering over,
the same bleached sky,

and when the officer calls me
it is a name I do not recognize,
a self I do not recognize.

We are asked to kneel, or
stand still, depending on which land
we embroider our feet with.

This one is copious with black blood
or so I am told.

Someone calls me by the skin
I did not know I had
and to this I think—language.

There must be a language
that contains us all
that contains all of this.

How do we disassemble
the sorrow of beginnings?

How do we let go, and not
crouch beneath other bodies?
How do we stop breathing, how *not* to?

Our fathers are not elders here;
they are long-bearded men
chauffeuring taxi cabs and sprawled
in small valet parking lots.

At their sight, my body dims its light
(a desiccated grape)
and murmurs, *Igziabher Yistilign*—
our pride, raw-purple again.

We begin like this: all of us
walking in solitude
walking a desert earth and
unforgiving bodies. We cross lines
we dare not speak of; we learn and
unlearn things quickly, or intentionally slow
(because, that, we can control)
and give ourselves new names
because these selves must be new
to forget the old blue.

But, sometimes, we also begin like this:
on a cold, cold night
memorizing escape routes,
kissing the foreheads of small children,
hiding *accat* in our pockets,
a rosary for safekeeping.

Or, married off to men thirty years our elders,
big house, big job, big, striking hands.

Or, thinking of the mouths to feed
many waters away.

At times
we also begin in silence;

water making its way into our bodies—
rain, or tears, or black and red seas
until we are ripe with longing.

Transcendence

She wears a hijab. She
wears *netela*. When she speaks
her tongue is molasses, honey,
enjera, *adey abeba*.

She runs twice as fast
apologizing for each child she's had,
and cannot have.

Her skin browns, henna drizzling
with the maps of ancient cities
she understands are found in her belly.

Before she gives birth
the specificity of things comes back to her—
how women are expected to always be strong,
like bone, like steel, unfractured,
not by will, but by necessity.

She thinks of the disappointment of a father
learning his firstborn is a girl,
how the little one will come to this world
unadorned—having her rights already claimed
by male siblings,

how the man who will later
kidnap and rape her
will have known her to be a child
and nothing more, and how
being the youngest wife
she will learn to succumb to his ways too.

She wishes the world
imagined more for her, even if a little bit.

But then she becomes a mother
and mother does not flinch
having trained her bones
not to break.

The strength of the Blue Nile
has taught her not to unravel
in front of men questioning her presence.

And when they call her flower, lotus, sunshine
she knows only this:

such names cannot contain
the transcendence of her strengths.

And so she calls herself water
and keeps her body from breaking open,

and when she finds herself by riverbanks
suddenly floating over Abbay

here, she says, here is my name:

I am more, I am free.

Black Thing

We wear these maps on our bodies,
filled with bone etchings,

one border made of woven hairs,
one fenced with golden teeth.

We stop to see the marrow of things—
and there, standing between us, the shadows

of our ghosts, the shadows of our ancestors,
waiting to carry us across
black, black seas littered with fury

silent still, headless bodies resembling ours
speaking the language of the silences we have grown
accustomed to. And this crossing,

like an ancient ritual, shows up everywhere we go,
every land we have fallen into.

We reveal our firmaments to them:

the breast where someone planted their flag,
the eye socket where we hid our mis-seeing,
the abdomens forced to heave, and retreat without a sound.

Here, we expose our unadorned
skin laced with golden things,

and ask, what made you, ancestor bodies,
what say you, of this black, black thing.

Cain

Here you are
now my brother, now
a stranger,

first son
of death.

Sometimes your eyes
are mine, your breath
mine, and this blood
in your hands too, mine.

To claim you
and parts of you
my biggest pride,
and sorrow.

I, my brother's keeper;
I, my brother's forfeiture.

This lamb I offered in sacrifice
is the last thing I see
before the light.

I see this, too:
shame arching your back
the sons of your sons
still running, still in hiding.

Brother, I do not recall
the killing, only days we spent
before the knowing, and
evenings under the stars,
and the world that refused
to acknowledge us anew.

Here you are, brother,
still with me, still my
flesh, my Cain.

Crossing Borders

When we left our homes,
someone set them on fire
though our eyes are trained to no longer
see this. Instead, this house,

we say, is filled with yellow daisies,
and its backyard houses the acacia tree
mother planted years ago.

We are given new names, new
sounds for our sorrows. We are
told new stories that somehow
still do not belong to us.

When we cross the borders
we hope both of us will make it,
though we know one won't.

Conversations are brief
and chopped; ordinary things
fill our mouths, washing the
sour taste of bleeding things.

The lands that grow beneath
our feet are on fire too, and here
we see ourselves reflected back.

The lines that separate us are many,
and many more we follow, or
hold, or hide until we see each other again—

in our sleeping, we become yellow daisies,
and mother the acacia tree housing us all.

Crackling Blue

The hand that feeds us bleeds
of things we do not know.
We call it mother, it gives us
names of things unsaid. When
we feast, small plants are born
from rivers, and spread like wild
flowers. Our eyes are little black suns.
We are told many things
we choose not to remember—
how to stand in silence, how to
bloom in complete darkness, how to
retrieve or be retrieved without our
knowing, how to understand invisibility.
The seeds we plant are many, but
many more of us grow—
these ones erect and unapologetic
small conquerors of old worlds—
though, they too, must carry the
weight of distraught ancestors
like heavy rocks, sinking into their bones
deeper and deeper
until their crackling turns blue.

Dreaming of Ethiopia

I feel this in my bones
but can't explain it to others,
or myself.

Thick with belonging,
raw from longing.

I dream of you
as if you are here,
or, as if I never left,

parts of me still scattered—
Addis, Bahir Dar, Lalibela, Aksum, Harar.

My fathers have warned me
about this, about you,
about all of it.

This land, like a loved one,
sneaks on me in the depth
of my solitude.

What do I do
with this dream?

Do I paint it in blue
and bathe myself in it;

do I bloom in its yellows
and reds and rich greens
and hang it above my walls;

do I let it go it
or carry it with me?

Everywhere I go
I am bent with the weight
of insurmountable loss.

Beneath Our Knowing
Lurk the Shadows of Men

To refer to my pre-pubescent body
as: *this*. This, and nothing else.

I later think of it
within the safety of geometric shapes;

a line here, another line here,
a dark corner there.

I dare not think of curves
or find myself in the midst
of unexplained wrath.

To have my first crush
described only as this: sex.

Nothing else attached to it,
or, the eyes of many men
lurking, lurking.

The first shadow, my father,
explains things to me
unknowingly.

This tenderness
confuses me years later.

This grayness that envelopes us,
a wild thing behind his irises,

is it love, is it not?

I was touched

in broad daylight,

something telling this child's body
of its sexual nature.

I ask friends,
where does one go
to get rid of it?

They laugh
and invite me behind bushes.

I have learned
the knowing that comes
from the touching;

the emptiness after.

Grandmothers

My grandmothers are made
of wool, each leading a caravan,
sitting upright on camels and dromedaries,
reading desert dunes like their palms.

A water they once knew
calls them by name;
each ululation, a renaming,
and with them, I stand or
sit, somewhere under
an acacia tree, or
an olive tree.

The grandmothers embrace
each other, a warmth I have
only dreamed about, and I
disappear among them
where we all become one,
and I lit, like fire, like
thunderstorm, memorize

our names, our stories, one by one

With the task of remembrance;
each story is carved carefully
into my bleeding skin; this
cut belonging to someone else,
this ache originating from
another body, having travelled
in the termite wounds of the Rift Valley.
This smoke, this crackling, perhaps
from a green river, or was it blue,
and this scream, at times quiet,
at times poised, opens us all at once.

I make a promise
I cannot keep, carrying with me
many sorrows, generations apart

giving them, giving us, names only we know:
flower, dust, dirt, dune, skin, algae,
sun, moon, fire—

the names I give each of my seeds
to plant them anew.

Mother Mango II

Mother is a mango-looking tree.
She bleeds from the inside out
until she is ripe and ready.

She calls us honey.
She feeds us fruit flies and fire-worms.
She lets us climb back into her womb
where it is quiet and safe.

At night, she calls us sweet thing.
We sweeten her womb, honey dripping
out until the early morning;
we are saccharine and tangy
like the winds of Danakil depressions.

At dawn, she calls us home, too,
though we do not know what that means
or how quickly we must forget its warmth.

Often times, the honeysuckle feeding us
dries deep within, then
we are told to adjust ourselves
within new boundaries.

Mother grows tall and orange;
everywhere she goes, a small
sun adorns new horizons.

The fruits of my fruit, she says,
are made with deep blue—
growing and shedding skins
(now black, now brown).

And these new lands
are like snakes with bellies of fire
ready to paint us with their venom.

War

I have been described by it, often
seen it rise up to the mouths of strangers,

as if to say, all things foreign—*note: referring
to me, or, my body, as a thing; an object*—are
made of war, or: things infested by war.

This thing, I also notice, comes within
language: that which we use to define

our own, or not; the knowing we choose
to acknowledge, that which we ignore.

This thing, is also a fruit. thorns on the outside,
bleeding meat on the inside, quenching
a thirst, a cry, nostalgia for simpler days.

War, I find, is also this: constant hiding,
home within invisibility, or worry, or

brokenness. Not knowing what to do
or say to the grief-stricken. Having to explain,
amidst tears, or bewilderment, the difference
between the immigrant, and the refugee. I am
inclined to think: wretched, once there, now

here—lost. The constant loss, coating our skin
like thin ash. Having to beg—*see me, see this*

humanness in me. The knowing about our new selves:
as an alien—*again, a thing, an object*. Having to count
our fears too; that of assimilation, that of

unbelonging, that of a new death, that of an imminent threat.

Knowing the gendered histories of our bodies,
and shaping a way to forgetfulness—to survive

this thing—*note here: not an object, but a*
constant self of being.

Wax & Gold

In ancient Aksum, I am told
I have ancestor queens—

mother Saba, and mother Gudit,
both without a king.

These and other mothers
birth me in water and fire,
sculpt me from mountain rocks
and breathe me into this life.

My fathers, too, stand in unison:
father Ezana, father Lalibela,
father Fasiledes.

In their arms, I am a first-born
or a first twin.

My fathers teach me how to speak,
my mothers how to survive.

With both, I am expected
to become a warrior,
or a monk.

My dreams are of other lands;

I travel to Jerusalem
to steal the Ark;

I bear sons
with the names of kings,

I become the mother
to other ancestor mothers.

This is what we know best:
how to sow sorrows like thick quilts
deep into our bones, how to speak
eloquently in all languages, starting with Geéz,
how to bear war in each hand, and shout
the names of the dead, or saints, or both.

We collect ourselves too,
so others do not see
the depth of our breaking.

Letters from America
Excerpts

I.

Dear [   ],

These days, I hide. I cannot [   ]
as I did before. What must you be
thinking of me?

This is not the first time I [   ],
but perhaps it might be the last.

I am told to stay strong, but when [   ]
speak, it's as if I am an infant with
no sorrow to muster.

I [   ] too, but
not always.

Sometimes I wake up with a [   ]
stuck on my chest, and
I can't [   ].

Sometimes I think you're not [   ]
but that's [   ] thinking.

Sometimes, I see you
in my [   ], or is it my [   ],
but then you [   ].

Must you [   ]
this fleeting?

II.

Dear [   ],

I read about you the other day,
on [   ], or was it [   ]?

I can't recall.
I can't recall much these days,
though I remember the way you [   ]
off, always [   ].

What were we thinking then?
The officer who took my [   ]
has your same dimples, and
I stared, and stared until they [   ] slowly.

I don't anymore.

III.

[   ] dear,

what [ ] when [   ] and [   ]?

Dear [   ],
I have not forgotten about you,

I am just [   ] and [   ]—

you knew this, didn't you?

Little Fires

I take these little fires
with me everywhere I go.

This one from Meskel
bright and blue and green all over,
sways on one foot, as if released
to a new world, one arm in flight,
one always catching upwards, upwards.

This from Addis Amet
its flame dark and ashen
still carries *kiremt* rain, still
smells of *puagume* and
hope and settled dust.

This one, I find in small heads,
adorning the black furs of Lalibela mountains,
one, two, many, forever resting in the mouths
of rock-hewn churches,
lighting our ways into solitude, into freedom.

This one from a lantern I leave unguarded,
smells of burned skin and slit wrists.

This one is pulled out from me
and turns into flesh and bones.

Wherever I go, these little fires
follow me: somber, brilliant and blue,
and I, a tossed thing, burning all over.

Water Ancestors

I.

Lately, I think a lot about my ancestors.
Ancestor mothers, ancestor fathers,
ancestor children. Perhaps it is because
they have come back to see me, one or
many at a time, carrying on their shoulders
the crisp blue waters of Abbay.

This, I feel inside me, as if
my blood is in fact blue-green.

I know it is.

I, at my best, am traveled water;
I have no resting place.

The lands I go to are all
different, and in them, I too
become someone else, sometimes
unrecognizable, but, at times,
despairingly assimilated.

And, as an immigrant, I find myself
thinking about shifting and moving;

and the breaking that occurs,
is both visible and invisible.

With this, something breaks
open too: the shifting of the self
into another one, the moving of the self
into many, the self as no one, the self
as new, impassible.

I, like many, I suspect, tell myself this:
there is nothing breaking here, nothing bleeding,
nothing festering to see.

How ordinary of me, to reassure myself
in such a complacent way.

Instead, I should be saying:
here, in this body, someone died,
perhaps not entirely, but bits and
pieces left here and there.

The further from my home,
the more the breaking.

When I am asked, where is home,
I say, which one?

The one that gave birth to me
and kicked me out, multiple times?
The one that calls me by a name
I do not recognize? The one that
claimed my tongue before I knew
its marred history? Or the one
that follows me everywhere I go,
small demon on my back,
a reminder incised deeply
into my bones.

These, and more,
home, and yet *not*.

II.

I carry them with me
wherever I go.

This ancestor who was promised in marriage
when she was three years old; this one
who ached to learn how to read and write,
but never did; this who found herself
among white men, and birthed children
with brown skin and blue eyes;
this who marries a woman that refuses
to give him children; this one, who is a
warrior king, last breath filled
with the smoke of a flying bullet;
this elegance who saw *Finfinne*
before it was so; and far beyond,
even further, this one, who traveled
many seas to collect the word of God.

These, and more,
I carry on my back,
and my body flattens itself.

So much history,
so little to unravel it with.

The dreams of my father
consume me.

My mother's too
are well-preserved,
small pockets
folded within my skin.

III.

I dream of home
and never live to see it.

The lands I inhabit
are filled with bones;
mine, my ancestor's
and my son's.

When I find myself in water,
the dread that devours me is not mine,
but perhaps yours, oh ancestor brother,
and the feeling of having crossed
many seas before is not new, either.

I come to Los Angeles
and find the devil
waiting on my doorstep;

and beneath the horizon
all is old and foreign to me.

My tongue betrays me many,
many times. It calls my name by another,
it changes its curls and whorls
to be released from its original accents.

These languages too, all coalesce
into chaos: blue, or black, or bleeding
burgundy, they are shadows, following me
everywhere I go.

I walk down the street, and hear myself saying,
hello, how are you, have a good day.

Where, does one go,
to have a good day?

IV.

The cities too, are grasslands
of bones and dust. Here I find
bits of others—a bit of Asmara,
a bit of Rome, a bit of Addis Ababa,
a bit of San Francisco; pieces for me
to mend. And when strangers ask,
where are you from, I say, hesitantly,
nowhere, nowhere.

V.

The stories I hold
are made of stones.

Some I throw under
the ocean's feet, hoping they will wash
away to a new land. Some I carry
in my pockets to keep me from
becoming invisible. Some, I'm afraid,
have replaced my eye sockets, and sit there,
waiting, waiting.

This waiting, slowly eats away
parts of me I did not know existed.

This skin sheds
like that of a snake's.

How many colors
are within me?

Black, brown,
blue, blood.

The wounds
of purple.

I muster the art of invisibility,
the requiem of solitude. In this,
I find comfort, because it won't ask me
to point towards home.

Home is where the bones
are buried, where the bodies laid bloated,
where the heads hung upside down,
where the smell of flesh is not new.

Home is also cruel;
why do we
forget that.

VI.

I am thinking
about water too.

Not the blue,
but black-green.

I must have been born
underneath the Blue Nile,
or have existed beneath
the bed of Lake Tana.

I feel it running in my veins,
as if it was light.

How many shadows
have to exist within me
before I know which light to follow—

VII.

In its best days, the Blue Nile
spits white, foaming sunlight
under its teeth.

Here we come to recount our sorrows,
our hopes, our dreams.

This water is wise, having traveled
many lands, having carried with itself
the voices of lost men and women,
having fed many.

It bleeds heavily;
perhaps it sees us,
our misgivings,
our small joys.

VIII.

I find definition
to be pleasing,
contained.

Water.

A colorless, transparent,
odorless, tasteless liquid
that forms the seas, lakes,
rivers, and rain,
and is the basis of the fluids
of living organisms.

In this, I can be contained.

§

Acknowledgments

Thank you to the editors of the following journals, where earlier versions of these poems appeared:

Poets.org: "Beginnings," "Nomenclatures of Invisibility";
Barrow Street Journal: "Lit";
Prairie Schooner: "Crossing Borders";
Visual Verse: "Crackling Blue";
World Literature Today: "Nomenclatures II," "Dust and Bones,"
      "*The Languages I Speak*," "Sawdust," "The Eucalyptus Tree I."

The poem "Wuchalle" owes its thinking and form to Layli Long Soldier's "Whereas." The poem "Mother Mango II" was inspired by Tsitsi Ella Jaji's "Family Tree."

Thank you to the African Poetry Book Fund for giving home to my earlier collections; in particularly, thank you to Kwame Dawes and Chris Abani, for your boundless generosity, for your seeing of new African voices, for the excellence, the care, and the impeccable work ethic you set for all of us; *Igziabher Yistilign*. Thank you to Aracelis Girmay, without whom this collection would not have found a home; thank you also brillante for your knowing, and your seeing, which brought forth my own. Thank you to Matthew Shenoda, for your generosity and your vast, vast mind; for holding this collection in your knowing light. Thank you to Dorianne Laux, for your sharp, sharp eye, and for being willing to bear this collection with new eyes. Thank you to the editors of *World Literature Today*, in particularly, thank you Daniel A. Simon and Michelle Johnson for trusting me with such an important platform, and allowing me to curate the Black Voices Series at a moment when such space of discernment was needed. Thank you to the wonderful folks at BOA Editions Ltd., for your care and support with this manuscript; thank you Michelle Dashevsky, thank you Peter Conners for giving this collection such a beautiful home. Thank you to my colleagues, friends and students at Pacific University. Thank you to my communities, my families, my people across lands, to whom this collection owes its thinking. Thank you to my Anaphora Arts community, that continues to bring joy and fellowship into my life. Thank you to my family, for enduring my woes and my wordlessness. Thank you God for all that is, and for all that isn't.

This watering is dedicated to Kokeb Zeleke, my ancestor-sister, artist, friend, soulmate. Love, love—Kokina.

Water Ancestors—what say you now? Have we reached the buoyancy you seek?

§

About the Author

Mahtem Shiferraw is a writer and visual artist from Ethiopia and Eritrea. She is the author of the chapbook *Behind Walls & Glass* (Finishing Line Press, 2015); *Fuchsia* (University of Nebraska Press, 2016), which won the Sillerman First Book Prize for African Poets; and *Your Body Is War* (University of Nebraska Press, 2018). Her work has been published in various literary journals, including *Prairie Schooner, World Literature Today, Diverse Voices Quarterly, Poets.org, Luna Luna Magazine, Barrow Street*, and more. She is the founder of Anaphora Arts, a nonprofit organization that advocates for writers and artists of color. She has served as a jury member for different literary prizes and residencies, including the Neudstat International Prize for Literature, the Brunel International African Poetry Prize, the Lucy Munro Brooker Prize, and more. She serves on the Editorial Board of *World Literature Today*, where she curated the Black Voices Series (2020, 2021), and the New African Voices Series (2022). She holds an MFA from Vermont College and teaches at Pacific University's low residency MFA program.

BOA Editions, Ltd. American Poets Continuum Series

Colophon

BOA Editions, Ltd., a not-for-profit publisher of poetry and other literary works, fosters readership and appreciation of contemporary literature. By identifying, cultivating, and publishing both new and established poets and selecting authors of unique literary talent, BOA brings high-quality literature to the public.

Support for this effort comes from the sale of its publications, grant funding, and private donations.

The publication of this book is made possible, in part, by the special support of the following individuals:

Anonymous

Blue Flower Arts, LLC

Angela Bonazinga & Catherine Lewis

Christopher C. Dahl

James Long Hale

Margaret B. Heminway

Grant Holcomb

Kathleen Holcombe

Nora A. Jones

Paul LaFerriere & Dorrie Parini, *in honor of Bill Waddell*

Barbara Lovenheim

Joe McEleveny

Nocon & Associates, a private wealth advisory practice of Ameriprise Financial Services LLC

Boo Poulin

John H. Schultz

William Waddell & Linda Rubel

Michael Waters & Mihaela Moscaliuc